HOW
SHARKS
AND OTHER ANIMALS
SENSE ELECTRICITY

Christine Honders

New York

Published in 2016 by The Rosen Publishing Group, Inc.
29 East 21st Street, New York, NY 10010

First Edition

Editor: Katie Kawa
Book Design: Reann Nye

Photo Credits: Cover Reinhard Dirscherl/WaterFrame/Getty Images; pp. 5, 14 Volt Collection/Shutterstock.com; p. 7 Willyam Bradberry/Shutterstock.com; p. 8 Mark Conlin/Oxford Scientific/Getty Images; p. 9 Pommeyrol Vincent/Shutterstock.com; p. 11 (shark) Alexius Sutandio/Shutterstock.com; p. 11 (skate) Andrew J Martinez/Science Souce/Getty Images; p. 13 Derek Heasley/Shutterstock.com; p. 17 (electric eel) Stacey Newman/Shutterstock.com; p. 17 (elephantnose fish) boban_nz/Shutterstock.com; p. 17 (sawfish) Auscape/UIG/Universal Images Group/Getty Images; p. 18 Dennis van de Water/Shutterstock.com; p. 19 worldswildlifewonders/Shutterstock.com; p. 20 wonderisland/Shutterstock.com; pp. 21, 22 frantisekhojdysz/Shutterstock.com.

Library of Congress Cataloging-in-Publication Data

Honders, Christine, author.
 How sharks and other animals sense electricity / Christine Honders.
    pages cm. — (Superior animal series)
Includes bibliographical references and index.
ISBN 978-1-4994-0994-9 (pbk.)
ISBN 978-1-4994-1032-7 (6 pack)
ISBN 978-1-4994-1074-7 (library binding)
1. Sharks—Juvenile literature. 2. Electrophysiology—Juvenile literature. 3. Senses and sensation—Juvenile literature. I. Title.
QL638.9.H66 2016
597.3—dc23

2015012730

Manufactured in the United States of America

CPSIA Compliance Information: Batch #WS15PK: For Further Information contact Rosen Publishing, New York, New York at 1-800-237-9932

CONTENTS

WIRED FOR HUNTING

Sharks have lived on Earth for about 400 million years. They're some of the world's best hunters. In fact, the earliest sharks hunted in Earth's oceans even before dinosaurs lived on Earth. Scientists think the sharks we see today swam in the oceans as dinosaurs walked on land.

One reason sharks are such good hunters is because they have amazing senses. They can smell a drop of blood in 25 gallons (95 l) of water. They also have a great sense of sight. However, their most amazing sense is something most animals don't have. Sharks sense electricity!

THAT MAKES SENSE!

Some sharks can smell blood in water up to 3 miles (5 km) away.

Great white sharks are the largest predatory fish, or fish that hunt other animals, in the ocean.

A SHARK'S SIXTH SENSE

All animals know they should stay away from sharks, especially smaller, weaker fish. No matter how they try to hide, though, sharks can find them. That's because sharks have the ability to sense electrical currents. This sixth sense is called electroreception.

All animals create electrical currents through their movements. The tiniest movement of muscles, a heartbeat, and even brain activity create electricity. Luckily for humans and other animals that live on land, electricity doesn't travel well through air. Fish that swim in salt water aren't so lucky. The **ions** in salt water have an electrical charge, which helps carry electricity through water.

THAT MAKES SENSE!

Fish create a different electrical charge than the ions around them, which creates a weak **voltage** in the water. Sharks can sense even the tiniest change in the water's voltage.

Electrical currents made by animals are natural and can't be controlled. Fish can't turn them off in order to stay safe from sharks.

Amazing Ampullae

In 1678, an Italian scientist named Stefano Lorenzini noticed that sharks had a bunch of pores, or tiny openings in the skin, all around their mouth. He saw that each pore opened into a long tube in the shark's body that's filled with a gel. He wasn't sure what the pores and tubes were for, and it was hundreds of years before anyone figured it out.

Scientists now know these pores are what allow sharks to sense electricity. Each pore's tube ends in a pouch connected to the shark's brain. Scientists named these sense **organs** ampullae of Lorenzini after the man who first discovered them.

THAT MAKES SENSE!

The number of pores on a shark's face is connected to how much the shark hunts. Active hunters, such as the hammerhead or tiger shark, can have 1,500 or more of these pores.

These tiny holes in the skin of a blue shark are the openings to the shark's ampullae of Lorenzini. Ampullae are pouches in an animal's body.

From the Ocean to the Brain

It would take until the 20th century before scientists discovered how these tubes and pores worked. The gel in the tubes is a conductor, which means electricity moves through it easily. Electrical currents travel through the gel to the bottom of the ampullae, which are covered with tiny hairs called cilia.

Humans have cilia in their ears, which tell the brain about noises when sound waves pass by them. When a fish swims close to a shark, it gives off an electrical current. The cilia respond to the current by sending a message to the shark's brain that something alive is nearby.

THAT MAKES SENSE!

Skates, which are another kind of fish with electroreception, have larger ampullae if they live in deeper water. They depend on electroreception to find food, because the bottom of the ocean is so dark that it's hard to see.

great white shark

Electroreception is an important sense for animals, such as sharks and skates, that live in dark ocean waters.

skate

Not only do sharks have the helpful h sense of electroreception, they have ther amazing ability that's known as r seventh sense. This sense allows rks to feel changes in the movement he water around them. It's controlled a part of the body called the lateral system.

The lateral line system is made up of g tubes that start at the head, near the ullae of Lorenzini. The tubes run down n side of the shark's body—just under skin—all the way to the tail. Along se main tubes are smaller tubes, which d to the surface of the shark's skin.

THAT MAKES SENSE!

When water flows around a large object, such as a huge rock, it changes direction. If a shark gets near that rock, the change in the water's movement is sensed by special cells, which tell the shark a large object is nearby.

The sensory cells in a shark's lateral line system are called neuromasts.

hammerhead shark

HOW SHARKS ATTACK

Electroreception and sharks' other senses make them some of the greatest hunters on Earth. While electroreception is amazing, it's not effective until the shark gets close to an electrical current. A shark's sense of smell is much better than a person's sense of smell, so it uses that first to find its **prey**. When it gets around 3 feet (0.9 m) away from its prey, electroreception takes over!

When great white sharks get ready to make their final attack, they roll their eyes to the back of their head to keep them safe. Then, they depend on electroreception to find and catch their next meal.

THAT MAKES SENSE!

Sharks sense the boats and electrical equipment, or gear, used by people before they sense the presence of actual humans in the water. This is because boats and electrical equipment create stronger electrical currents than the human body.

GREAT WHITE SHARK SENSES

SENSE	WHAT'S SPECIAL ABOUT IT?
sight	A shark's eye is split into two areas: one for seeing during the day and one for seeing at night. Sharks can see much better in darkness than people can.
smell	A shark's strongest sense is its sense of smell. It can smell one drop of blood in 10 billion drops of water.
taste	Sharks have taste buds that can identify food before they eat it.
touch	Sharks can feel changes in temperature, or how hot or cold the water around them is.
hearing	Sharks have small ears that are good at picking up low sounds in the water.
electroreception	Sharks can sense the electrical currents produced by the body of their prey.
movement	Sharks use their lateral line system to sense the direction and amount of movement in the water around them.

Sharks aren't the only animals in the ocean that have electroreception. Skates and rays also have this sixth sense. They belong to the same group of animals as sharks. Animals in this group are called elasmobranchs. Elasmobranchs have a **skeleton** made of **cartilage** instead of bone.

Sawfish are another kind of elasmobranch. Sawfish live at the bottom of the ocean and have a long snout that looks like a saw. A sawfish's snout is covered with electroreceptors, or electricity-sensing cells. This helps find sea animals to eat. After sawfish find their prey, they use their special snout to attack.

THAT MAKES SENSE!

Some fish create more electricity than others. Electric eels constantly make small amounts of electricity to find their way around in the water. If they feel they're in danger, they quickly give their attacker a high-voltage shock!

electric eel

elephantnose fish

Elephantnose fish find food and get around the ocean by making electrical currents with their tail and sensing any changes to that current. They can tell the difference between living and dead bugs buried in the ocean sand.

sawfish

OTHER SHOCKING ANIMALS

Few **mammals** can sense electrical currents because electricity doesn't travel well through air. A platypus lives on both land and water. It needs electroreception to catch its prey because it swims with its ears, eyes, and nostrils closed. A platypus's duck-like bill is covered in nearly 40,000 electroreceptors.

An echidna is another kind of mammal that has electroreceptors on the end of its snout. Echidnas are also known as spiny anteaters. Long-beaked echidnas live in forests and use their electroreceptors to find worms buried in leaves. Short-beaked echidnas feed on ants and termites living in nests, which they find using their electroreceptors.

oriental hornet

A platypus has thousands more electroreceptors on its snout than an echidna.

platypus

THAT MAKES SENSE!

Oriental hornets are active during the hottest times of day, and their body traps sunlight and turns it into electricity.

The Internet allows people to get **information** from all over the world. That's possible because of undersea cables. Undersea cables are wires buried in the ocean floor that connect every part of the world to the Internet. In fact, 99 percent of Internet **communication** between the United States and other countries is carried by undersea cables. While this is a great thing for people, it can confuse sharks.

Undersea cables create electrical currents. If a shark swims close to an undersea cable and senses this electricity, it may bite the cable thinking it's a fish.

Pollution of the ocean by people is also harmful to shark senses.

THAT MAKES SENSE!

If a shark bites an undersea cable, it could cause big problems for Internet connections in some parts of the world. Companies are working to come up with new cables that won't break if a shark bites them.

SUPERIOR SHARK SENSES

When people think of sharks, they often think of danger. They think sharks like to attack people. However, shark attacks don't happen very often. Sharks don't want to eat people. In fact, most shark bites happen when a shark thinks a person is a fish. When they sense they've bitten a person, they often let the person go.

Sharks are known for their strong senses. Their senses of smell, hearing, and sight are much more powerful than human senses. However, nothing is more amazing than their ability to sense electricity!

GLOSSARY

cartilage: A strong but bendable material found in some parts of the body.

communication: The act of sharing ideas, thoughts, or feelings with someone else.

information: Knowledge or facts about something.

ion: An atom or group of atoms that has a positive or negative charge due to losing or gaining an electron, or negative particle.

mammal: Any warm-blooded animal whose babies drink milk and whose body is covered with hair or fur.

organ: A body part that does a specific job.

prey: An animal hunted by other animals for food.

skeleton: The system of bones or cartilage that supports an animal's body.

snout: A body part that incudes the nose and jaws.

voltage: The force of an electrical current.

INDEX

WEBSITES

Due to the changing nature of Internet links, PowerKids Press has developed an online list of websites related to the subject of this book. This site is updated regularly. Please use this link to access the list: www.powerkidslinks.com/sas/shark